READING POWER

In the Ring with Goldberg

Michael Payan

The Rosen Publishing Group's
PowerKids Press ™
New York

1

To Di...Eight years of friendship and wackiness...who would've thought?

Published in 2002 by The Rosen Publishing Group, Inc.
29 East 21st Street, New York, NY 10010

First Edition

Book Design: Michael Donnellan

Photo Credits: All photos by Colin Bowman

Payan, Michael.
In the ring with Goldberg / Michael Payan.
   p. cm. — (Wrestlers)
Includes bibliographical references (p.) and index.
ISBN 0-8239-6046-3
1. Goldberg, Bill, 1966– —Juvenile literature. 2. Wrestlers—United States—Biography—Juvenile literature. [1. Goldberg, Bill, 1966– 2. Wrestlers.] I. Title.
 GV1196.G65 P39 2002
 796.812'092-dc21

                                                          00-013037

Manufactured in the United States of America

Contents

Goldberg is a wrestler.
He is very strong.

Goldberg shakes the hands of his fans before his match. He has lots of fans.

Goldberg appears through smoke and fireworks.

9

Goldberg is in the
ring with his opponent.
Goldberg makes his move.

Goldberg is backed into a corner. He pushes his opponent.

Goldberg lifts Horace
on his shoulders.

Goldberg squeezes
Scott Steiner's head.

Goldberg sits on
Kevin Nash.

Goldberg wins.
He raises his hands
in victory.

Glossary

fans (FANZ) People who admire an athlete or celebrity.

opponent (uh-POH-nent) A person who is on the opposite side in a game or match.

ring (RING) A square shaped enclosed area where a wrestling match takes place.

victory (VIK-tor-ee) To have success over your opponent, to win.

Here is another book to read
about Goldberg:

Bill Goldberg (Prowrestling Stars)
by Kyle Alexander.
Paperback (March 2000)

For more information about Goldberg,
check out these Web sites:

www.wcwwrestling.com/2001/
  superstars/billgoldberg/
www.geocities.com/colosseum/
  bench/5286/

Index

Word Count: 75

Note to Librarians, Teachers, and Parents

If reading is a challenge, Reading Power is a solution! Reading Power is perfect for readers who want high-interest subject matter at an accessible reading level. These fact-filled, photo-illustrated books are designed for readers who want straightforward vocabulary, engaging topics, and a manageable reading experience. With clear picture/text correspondence, leveled Reading Power books put the reader in charge. Now readers have the power to get the information they want and the skills they need in a user-friendly format.